EMPOWERING BELIEF

Debra Sweeting

TABLE OF CONTENTS

Chapter One: My Story ... 1
Chapter Two: The "ifs" in Life ... 7
Chapter Three: Things We Can Control ... 13
Chapter Four: Embrace Your Deficiencies ... 19
Chapter Five: Faith Requires Patience ... 25
Chapter Six: That Moment of Change ... 31
Chapter Seven: Science Has Shown Us ... 37
Chapter Eight: The Self-Confidence Formula ... 43
Chapter Nine: Repetition ... 49
Chapter Ten: Redemption Story ... 55
Chapter Eleven: The Wheel Of Life ... 63
Chapter Twelve: The Pen Is Mightier Than The Sword ... 71
Chapter Thirteen: Survive vs Thrive ... 77
Chapter Fourteen: I Forgive Myself ... 83
Chapter Fifteen: Imagination ... 89
Chapter Sixteen: The Law of Replacement Principle ... 97
Chapter Seventeen: Powerful Lessons Learned ... 103
Chapter Eighteen: Brokenness Is Beautiful in Gods Eyes ... 107

CHAPTER ONE

MY STORY

To say 2020 has been life-altering would not be an understatement! It feels as if each day of 2020 the COVID-19 pandemic has programmed worry, anxiety, fear, and uncertainty into our minds. Despite my efforts to quarantine, virtual school my daughter, and stock up on essentials to stay safe; 2020 had something equally devasting and life-altering instore for me. As they say, there is never a good time for bad news. However, getting a breast cancer diagnosis during a global pandemic takes the cake. During an already high stress time, additional thoughts of fear, uncertainty, and panic, came to mind. This diagnosis means surgery, chemotherapy, possibly a mastectomy, breast reconstruction and, a weakened immune system during a global pandemic that affects your respiratory system.

I am still undergoing chemotherapy as I write this book, but I am claiming TRIUMPH. In order to grow your belief on this journey to healing and success you will have to tell yourself a LIE that is the TRUTH. It says it in the word "BELIEF". Remove the first two letters BE and the last letter F and the word LIE remains. Right now, in my current state I am going through a sickness, however I must tell myself that I AM HEALED. In the natural it may be a lie but, in the Spirit, it is the TRUTH. Am I perfect at it, not at all but I can strive for perfection. Having an unshakeable belief system is not a destination. This is a journey of becoming all that God is asking you to become by using your faith. You are going to have moments where what happens to you physically affects you emotionally but then you always must remember that your words can speak life or death. How I am feeling, what I am visualizing has the ability to change what it is that I experience in the natural or physical world.

Mastering your emotions starts with mastering your words. What do I want to feel right now? Feelings come from the words we speak, the words we hear, the images we see, and the associations which create emotions. Once you have identified how you want to feel, the next step is to create the words that affirm how you want to feel in present statements: I am loved, my life is fulfilled, I am healed.

In my heart, I know that God prepared me for this part

FAITH IS ASSURANCE OF THINGS HOPED FOR, THE CONVICTION OF THINGS UNSEEN.

HEBREWS 11:1

of my journey. My daughter is safe at home with me. My parents to include my mother, father and stepmom referred to as mom provide insurmountable support. In addition, I closed on a new construction lake front home in June. Then after getting settled, I was diagnosed with breast cancer in September 2020.

Looking back at my level of faith, I had to check myself for the way that I react to things perceived as bad news. Worrying about everything outside of my control, allowing negative thoughts of "what if" to creep in, wondering if something would happen instead of just BELIEVING that God has already planned to use this situation to glorify his greatness. My mother always says, "today is today. We can only see what is in front of us, but God is limitless. He is all knowing. God is ready willing and more than capable of making miracles happen. All we must do is trust Him and believe with unwavering faith that things will manifest the way it is intended to". She is right, look how God answered one of my big prayers right before the additional stress of my diagnosis. He did not just provide my need for a new home but included my wants as a bonus. That was Gods way of saying the home I provided for you and Alana is just the beginning. At this point, I only needed to focus on God and my recovery from breast cancer. In life, it is not what happens to you but how you respond to what happens to you that makes the difference. After the initial shock and fear of being diagnosed with cancer for the second time in my life, I had to strengthen my faith over my fear which required lots of prayer! Assurance of things hoped for, the conviction of things unseen. Hebrews 11:1

MY STORY

An ah-ha moment for me is when I truly understood your physical world is created in the spiritual world, that is when my life changed. In other words, what takes place on the spiritual level is tied to what manifest in the physical level. Be means in the state of, lieve means loved by God, believe. I am loved by the words I am speaking. Be in the state of, life means glad. Belief means be in the state of being glad. This is how you expand your belief system.

You may have financial difficulty right now; however, you must tell yourself I AM RICH. In the natural that is a lie but, in the Spirit, it is the TRUTH. Everything could be falling apart in your life, however you must tell yourself I AM BLESSED, EVERYTHING IS WORKING OUT FOR MY GOOD. In the natural is does not feel or look like it but, in the Spirit, in His world, it is the truth. During your darkest hours, you must speak that lie that is the TRUTH. I have learned to speak life to every troubled situation in my life. You must speak light into every dark place in our life. You will live a prosperous victorious life because that is the whole TRUTH and nothing but the TRUTH as long as you believe. Through my empowering belief system, I experience a greater sense of purpose, energy, and moral authority that what is happening to me has great opportunity to birth something beautiful, purposeful in your honor, God.

EMPOWERING BELIEF

CHAPTER TWO

THE "IFS" IN LIFE

There are a lot of if's in life. Remove the "l" and "e" and you are left with the word IF. Life is a journey we must not only go through but grow through. It is important to silence the IF's in your mind. Therefore, we must develop an empowering belief system an unshakeable knowing of the power that exists inside of you. Trials and tribulations are a part of the rotating wheel of life. A lot of the things that happen in our lives are caused by what we attract, which encompasses both bad and good. Whatever you speak has a way of manifesting itself. The tongue is powerful. The mind is powerful. If you say, "My life sucks! I never get good breaks. This brings me bad luck.

I do not have the ability to achieve that amount of success. I have always had a hard life," guess what? That is exactly what you will manifest in your life. Whatever you believe is what you will be blessed with. You have the power to speak limitations and blessings into your life.

So, ask yourself, what are the mountains I need to move now? After plugging into many motivational personal development programs, I learned that failure is a necessary part of life. I have failed many times in my life and, yes, I felt sorry for myself, yes, I cried, I even blamed other people for my failures and then one day I realized that I needed to look in the mirror and take 100% responsibility for my life. It was time to move on from psychological barriers and grasp that every failure is an opportunity for growth. Knowledge is powerful to personal development.

We must accept the things we cannot change and courageously change the things that we can. The Serenity Prayer was written in the 1800's and embodies a deep-seated understanding of the relationship between humans, God and faith. The Serenity Prayer says, "God grant me the serenity to accept the things that I cannot change, the courage to change the things that I can and the wisdom to know the difference." Almost everyone on the planet has heard one version or another of this prayer however I am not sure everyone understands how powerfully impactful the message behind it is. The prayer is about strengthening your faith. It does not say, God help me to accept the stuff that I agree with, change the other stuff that I do not want to deal with and know the difference between the two. The prayer does say, "grant me the serenity to accept the

YOU HAVE THE POWER TO SPEAK LIMITATIONS AND BLESSINGS INTO YOUR LIFE. I CHOOSE BLESSINGS!

stuff that I cannot change." Serenity means calm, peaceful, untroubled. The point is, you can still accept that which we cannot change in your life without it worrying, angering, or frustrating you. Serenity is the key component to faith. The prayer goes on to ask for courage for the things that I can change. Courage is difficult and change is scary. This means that we need to confront things in ourselves that up until this point, we have been afraid to confront. You must be courageous in your faith as you grow and evolve on this journey. Be courageous in the face of unavoidable change and Lord grant me the wisdom to know the difference. Wisdom is knowing the difference so our efforts can be concentrated solely on the areas that can be more sustainable, reliable and worth the outcomes. Let us go forward in faith and love.

THE "IFS" IN LIFE

EMPOWERING BELIEF

CHAPTER THREE

THINGS WE CAN CONTROL

Now more than ever, you need to know how to stay focused on the desires of your heart and protect your energy. It is time to create epic beliefs to not just survive but thrive during and after this global pandemic is all over. To do this, we must focus on the things we can control while being quarantined. The first is, we can control our energy and vibration. Your mind, body and soul are composed purely of energy. For this reason, what you feel translates into how you feel. By raising your vibration or energy level, you can realign yourself with good health, peace of mind, and the ultimate truth of your potential.

We can control what you listen to. Music is capable of rousing both physiological emotions and responses. Adding podcasts into your day can be a great way to gain new knowledge and perspective in your faith, spirituality, finances, relationships, health, and emotional intelligence. It is important not to forget the power of silence. Give yourself time to be alone with your thoughts.

We can control what we watch. The content on television programs and social media can negatively affect your psychological health. It can do this by affecting your mood, and your mood can then affect aspects of your thinking and behavior.

We can control our emotions. Practicing gratitude and love involves taking time to notice and reflect upon the things you are thankful for. This in turn helps you experience more positive emotions, feel happier, feel more alive, sleep better, express more kindness and compassion and these positive thoughts can even positively affect your immune system.

We can live in the spirit of generosity. When we embody an attitude of generosity by giving of our time and resources to others, the good things we share expand from deep within our hearts as an offering of freedom from fear. Fear of not having enough, fear of not being enough and fear of rejection.

We can learn to stay focused and keep building our dreams. It takes consistency and disciplined focus under ordinary circumstances. Unfortunately, we are now living in a time that is truly unprecedented, unchartered territory from anything we have experienced before. Therefor the proper techniques and strategies of creating structure and self-care can help build your productivity while lowering your stress.

BY RAISING YOUR VIBRATION OR ENERGY LEVEL, YOU CAN REALIGN YOURSELF WITH GOOD HEALTH, PEACE OF MIND, AND THE ULTIMATE TRUTH OF YOUR POTENTIAL.

We can work out daily. Home workouts have become more popular now than ever before. There are plenty of ways to get an intense exercise session right in your living room. The objective is to start moving your body enough to get your heart rate elevated and work up a sweat daily. Many experts have written on the benefits of doing so.

We can eat healthy foods. My doctor recommended intermittent fasting for me. Creating an eating pattern where you have a meal or snack approximately every three hours can prevent mindless snacking with junk foods. Buy food that comes from the earth like vegetables, fruits, nuts, seeds, whole grains, and lean proteins. Stop buying processed foods such as chips and cookies. If you do not buy it, you cannot eat it.

We can hydrate our bodies with water. I read it is recommended to drink half your body weight in water. So, if you weigh 130 pounds, you will need to drink at least 64 ounces of water daily. I personally need a little flavor added to my water to reach my hydration goals. So, I typically add lemon, cucumbers, mint, and sometimes ginger to flavor things up a bit. The goal is to avoid sodas and beverages filled with sugar.

Lastly, we can create time for prayer. We can go a step further and create a space in your home for prayer as well. The bible says "But when you pray, go into your room, close the door and pray to your Father, who is unseen. Then your Father, who sees what is done in secret, will reward you." Mathew 6:6. Quarantine provides us with an opportunity to spend time reading scriptures independently and as a family. In addition to reading, you can meditate to reflect on what the scripture means and contemplate by using your imagination to become a participant by putting yourself in the story. Ultimately, deliberately putting time aside to spend with God is the best way to develop the consistent habit of incorporating Him into your schedule daily.

EMPOWERING BELIEF

CHAPTER FOUR

EMBRACE YOUR DEFICIENCIES

In a world plagued by the need for instant gratification it is more important to take stock of where we are in our journey towards success. Through patience, persistence and faith remember to focus not on big shifts but on small incremental changes applied diligently and continuously.

In society deficiencies are perceived as a negative character trait. The beauty industry was built entirely on the idea of perfection that profits on the self-deprivation and suffering of others. Look at the television or on social media and feel the pressure of those images of perfection. When people feel they are not perfect, not good enough or lacking in anyway than it is easy to sell them a surface level fix for some short-term relief.

The truth is, in the eyes of God we are all perfect, whole, and complete because He made us in his likeness, and He is the only one who is perfect. That means we are perfect in our imperfections. Perhaps we could also learn a lesson from the Japanese people.

I have a lot of respect for the Japanese culture, which is known for embracing history, language, cultural heritage, tradition, etiquette, herbal teas, arts and crafts, delicious foods, you name it. In addition, the Japanese culture has mastered the art of seeing value in brokenness. Kintsugi is a 400-year-old Japanese technique used to repair broken ceramics by highlighting the cracks with a special gold, silver, or platinum lacquer as part of the design. Many of us break dishes or other ceramics and discard it as trash without a second thought. However, the Japanese technique encourages a different mindset, one that sees the potential for reconstructing the broken pieces into a stronger even more uniquely beautiful piece of art – Kintsugi.

This technique is a relevant and powerful metaphor for embracing the mental, physical, and emotional scars we encounter along life's journey. 2020 is the 5th anniversary of my husband's death. I often see myself as broken, not enough to handle all the challenges that life throws my way. This personal tragedy for my daughter and I was one of the hardest things we have ever experienced. The grief is still exceedingly difficult at times.

The relevance of the Kintsugi technique occurred to me, it was a new way of visually seeing myself and my past experiences

THROUGH PATIENCE, PERSISTENCE AND FAITH REMEMBER TO FOCUS NOT ON BIG SHIFTS BUT ON SMALL INCREMENTAL CHANGES APPLIED DILIGENTLY AND CONTINUOUSLY.

This book fully embraces turning the mess life has dealt me into my message of redemption, hope, and healing to inspire someone else not to give up. Kintsugi is a powerful metaphor to understand the art of healing, being broken and carefully put back together again by the hands of God through prayer. I envision how much stronger I am and uniquely beautiful inside and out because of the lessons I have learned through hardships experienced. It is a powerful way to view yourself as the victor of your circumstances instead of flawed victim. This practice of having the mindset of becoming more resilient and even stronger after experiencing the death of a loved one, loss of a job, and cancer diagnosis is what many of us need.

As I read my bible and spend time with God, I learned God sees our potential for good and how our broken vessels can fulfill His ultimate purpose for our own and even someone else's life. It is a natural human response to be afraid or lacking in some way, but God works with each of us where we are currently, and He equips each of us to overcome our flaws and become what he wants us to be. We must surrender, let go of the excuses and see ourselves the way God sees us.

You are probably asking yourself how do I do that? You start by embracing your deficiencies. Take one of the things the media and society have used to make you feel less than and turn it around by making it your strength. It is not an accident that tv shows are called programs. If you sit in front of the television or social media repetitively day after day, it will program your mind into thinking that you are not enough. The cycle just continues and continues. Unfortunately, the behavior of becoming distracted from your goals in front of the television

EMBRACE YOUR DEFICIENCIES

is passed on from generation to generation, drowning oneself in inadequacies. So, what do successful people do differently? Instead of looking for the surface level quick fix of buying a big screen television, they buy a book. Instead of getting lost for hour on Facebook, Instagram, Snapchat and Ticktock, they get lost for hours reading or listening to empowering mind changing audio. This is the time to own your short comings, embrace your deficiencies which are the things you are not good at and instantly you will claim power over it, but the key is to be persistent and consistent.

EMPOWERING BELIEF

CHAPTER FIVE

FAITH REQUIRES PATIENCE

A farmer sowed his seeds all over the place. Some seeds fell on a path with no soil. Some on rocky ground, some on grassy lands grazed by wildlife for food. In the first three cases the seeds were taken away or failed to produce a crop but when it fell on good soil it grew yielding 100-fold. This is an example of Desire + Skills x Faith = Success which is the Success Formula. Faith is the single most important aspect of the formula and therefore the path to our dreams. As in multiplication, anything multiplied by zero will yield zero. All the skills in the world will add up to nothing if you do not have faith. Similarly, to how the farmer must continuously tend to his crops, we must plant the seed of patience and continually nurture success. Faith is the patience that allows you to always keep where you are going right in front of you. No matter what the ups and downs of life may bring that you are experiencing in that moment. People who give up on their dreams tend to do so when too much time passes. But time is not something God operates on. People operate on time. God operates on His word and we can learn to operate on the word when we say right now is the time to work on my dreams regardless of what is happening in the world or the trials and tribulations we currently face. Faith is patience that works through love. In love there is no jealousy or competition. Patient love is unconditional. Faith is unconditional.

Faith is your success plan towards having your desires met but through patience, love, and resilience you maintain your faith. Faith always rewards us with exactly what we put out to the world. If you think about how you felt over any given time, you will notice what has come back to you now or in the past is a direct reflection of the word you sent out to the world and the actions you followed up with.

As with everything we create and put into action, the seeds of thought are the words we use to first create our desires mentally before it manifests in the natural. With that being said, the most important words we use are said to yourself. So, knowing how to positively change your self-taught language is critical if we are pursuing a life of growth and success. Desire plus skill multiplied by faith is the formula for success that works every time. If you ever got less than what you wish for than maybe your desire was on point, but you did not apply

DESIRE PLUS SKILL MULTIPLIED BY FAITH IS THE FORMULA FOR SUCCESS THAT WORKS EVERY TIME!

the skills required to make it happen. Perhaps your skills were on point, but your desires could not get into your heart. Faith will increase your confidence and your confidence will in turn fuel your faith. It is a self-fulfilling cycle so always keep where you are going right in front of you.

It is time to step out on faith. Not faith in yourself, not faith in your lover, family, mentors, friends, business partners etc. Step out on faith in GOD. He is the truth and the light. I am not perfect. I reference God because he is perfect. The knowledge in this book is shared out of love in hopes of helping to transform lives all over the world.

FAITH REQUIRES PATIENCE

EMPOWERING BELIEF

CHAPTER SIX

THAT MOMENT OF CHANGE

I found myself feeling as though my life had hit rock bottom. Everything that I counted on as a form of stability was gone. I have grown in my spiritual life by paying closer attention to my internal conviction, in other words my intuition. Things that disturb and warn my soul to have caution, make good choices. I constantly speak to God seeking his will. I have lost the desire to do some of the old carnal actions of my past.

The bible says that God wants to dwell among his people. Therefore, I wanted to understand how I could develop a relationship with my Lord and Savior. The first thing I did was pour out my heart to God in prayer personally inviting him into my life.

Dear God, I need you, I am humbly crying out to you. I am tired of doing things my way. Help me to start doing things your way. I invite you into my life and my daughter's life to be our Lord and Savior. Fill the emptiness in me with your Holy Spirit and make me whole, Lord help me to trust and rely on you. Help me to know and love you. Help me to live for you. Help me to understand your grace, your mercy, and your peace. Thank you, Lord. Amen.

There is a saying that we are born without a manual. I believe this saying is false. God the creator of the heavens and earth also created the bible as a manual of how we should live to receive salvation. The Ten Commandments address the basic biblical laws of the bible. Exodus 20:3-17

No other gods before God The Father

No carved idol worshiping of earthly things in place of God

No taking Gods name in vain

Keep the Sabbath Day holy

Honor your parents

No killing (murder)

No adultery

No stealing

No bearing false witness which means (lying)

No coveting meaning do not envy people or what they own

The first four commandments are about supreme devotion to God and the final six commandments speak of a sincere

PAY CLOSER ATTENTION TO YOUR INTERNAL CONVICTION, IN OTHER WORDS THAT SOFT VOICE IN YOUR EAR AND IN YOUR SOUL.

affection for others. The purpose of this Law was to make it clear that as man who was born in sin, we could never match God's standards for holiness. Therefore, we must seek salvation through Christ. God wants to deliver each of us from the bondage and mental burden of our sin and take His rightful place at the very center of our lives.

Hitting your own rock bottom and saying enough is enough to yourself. Feelings of humiliation, anger to the point where you say that is it, I am done! Moving forward I am raising my standard; I will no longer live this way. I am better than this and I am now living Gods way. What is your rock bottom?

THAT MOMENT OF CHANGE

EMPOWERING BELIEF

CHAPTER SEVEN

SCIENCE HAS SHOWN US

The statistics around successful goal setting have been around since the 1950's. Science has shown us that written goals go hand in hand with success for decades. Only 3 percent of the population write down their goals. Yet ninety-five percent of all the successful people around the world have written goals. Coincidence? Probably not! So why aren't majority of us writing our goals down? Many of the people with goals still do not achieve the goals they have set for themselves. In fact, only 8 percent of all the people in the world who have goals actually hit the targets of the goals they have set. There is good news! Science has shown us seven things that successful people specifically do that guarantees success. First, they start with the end in mind. It is one of Stephen Covey's 7 Habits of Highly Successful People and it is a simple tool that has stood the test of time. Second, they build a support system around themselves. "If you go alone, you go fast but if we go with others we go far." David Imonitie

Third, they set goals that are specific, measurable, achievable, realistic, and timely (SMART). If your goals are too easy you procrastinate. If it is too hard, we become overwhelmed. The fourth trait is they recognize when they are procrastinating. We all suffer from procrastination in one form or another which is why it is important to recognize when you do it and implement techniques to overcome it. The fifth trait is mastering your time and often referred to as interval training in the sports arena. It is funny how the sports and business worlds often align when it comes to motivation and productivity training. In their working day, successful people follow a productivity schedule for maximum productivity such as a 25 minutes on 15 minutes off process, time blocking or the MIT method of completing your most important task first etc. The sixth trait is music which is a great way to maintain focus and stay positive during your goal attainment. The final trait is successful people do not multitask. Multitasking is a myth because the brain can only do one thing optimally well at a time. People who claim to be good at multitasking are just rapidly jumping between tasks and doing each of them a little bit more ineffectively the more they add on. So now that you know the secret sauce, each of these high achievement habits should become a part of your daily success habits.

SCIENCE HAS SHOWN US

"IF YOU GO ALONE, YOU GO FAST BUT IF WE GO WITH OTHERS WE GO FAR."
- DAVID IMONITIE

Father God, today I am grateful for the knowledge that has been prepared for me that I do not already know. I will learn, grow, and implement this information into my daily life. Amen!

SCIENCE HAS SHOWN US

EMPOWERING BELIEF

CHAPTER EIGHT

THE SELF-CONFIDENCE FORMULA

The self-confidence formula is a five-paragraph declaration in which Napoleon Hill challenges you to devote 10 minutes per day developing your self-confidence. David Imonitie introduced me to this declaration that I now incorporate into my daily success habits. I will explain how to apply this declaration in your life the way that it was explained step by step to me.

"I know that I have the ability to achieve the object of my Definite Purpose in life," It is imperative to know your definite purpose here on earth? For me, my definite purpose is to positively impact the lives of people through sharing my experiences and transformational strategies learned.

"I realize the dominating thoughts of my mind will eventually reproduce themselves outward, physical action, and gradually transform themselves into physical reality, I will concentrate my thoughts for thirty minutes daily, upon the task of thinking of the person I intend to become, thereby creating in my mind a clear mental picture of that person." This is saying, your dominating thoughts or your heart's desire will eventually reproduce themselves in an outward physical action. Something cannot be reproduced until it is first produced. Where is it produced? Your hearts desires are first produced in your mind. Anything that shows up in the physical was first created in the mind. The mind controls the body. Humans are made up of three parts: the mind, the spirit or soul and the body. The body follows the spirit and mind. It will gradually transform itself into physical reality. The key word here is gradually. Everyone wants instant success, but success is not overnight! I will concentrate my thoughts for 30 minutes daily upon the task of thinking about the person who I am becoming. The question here is, who am I becoming? Thereby in my mind creating a clear mental picture of that person.

"I know through the principle of auto-suggestion, any desire that I persistently hold in my mind will eventually seek expression through some practical means of attaining the object back of it, therefore, I will devote 10 minutes daily to demanding of myself the development of self-confidence." So, any desire that you consistently hold in your mind refers to that financial goal, business, people, opportunities, relationships, will seek expression meaning to go in pursuit of or in search of some practical means. Practical means refers to an idea, project, or opportunity capable of being done or put into effect. Therefore, I will devote 10 minutes daily to demanding of myself the development of self-confidence. This declaration is only demanding you commit 10 minutes daily to the development of your self-confidence. We are given 24 hours in a day. I feel strongly that everyone can find 10 minutes throughout their day to devote to their own personal growth development.

"I have clearly written down a description of my definite chief aim in life, and I will never stop trying until I shall have developed sufficient self-confidence for its attainment." Write it down and make it plain. Habakkuk 2:2-3 Think with the end result in mind. I was taught to go as far as creating a flyer for my next goal attainment. My mentor understands the importance of visually seeing your goals in front of you. The eyes do not know the difference. Remove the first "e" in the word eyes and you are left with the word "yes". Your eyes will start to tell your mind yes to your goal attainment.

"I fully realize that no wealth or position can long endure, unless built upon truth and justice, therefore I will engage in no transaction which does not benefit all whom it affects." This part is imperative! You have got to do things the right way! We have all seen people rise and fall because they chose to do things with dishonesty. It also says, if the transaction does not benefit everybody, do not engage in it. "I will succeed by attracting to myself the forces I wish to use, and the cooperation of other people." None of us can do this alone, we all need other people. "I will induce others to serve me, because of my willingness to serve others. I will eliminate hatred, envy, jealousy, selfishness, and cynicism, by developing love for all humanity, because I know that a negative attitude towards others can never bring me success." Okay, this is a get real moment! It is a natural human instinct to harbor feelings of hatred, jealousy, or envy. Simply put, we must stop the hatred! It clearly says having a negative attitude can never bring me success! When we exercise gratitude and celebrate the success of others all your doing is attracting success into your life by developing love for all of humanity. Faith comes by hearing, but faith works through love in your heart. "I will cause others to believe in me, because I will believe in them, and in myself." The message here is to lift others up. See how you can help them and encourage them whether they benefit you financially or in any other way or not. This declaration is incredibly powerful!

Lastly, it ends by requesting you to sign your name to this formula, "commit it to memory, and repeat it aloud once a day, with full faith that it will gradually influence your thoughts and actions so that you will become a self-reliant, and successful person." I personally have this declaration signed, laminated, and posted up on my wall so I can see it in front of me daily. I am so grateful to my mentor for introducing it to me. You don't know what you don't know until you do meaning everyone needs a mentor, someone who can share new insight and knowledge to help you to grow personally and professionally. Who is your mentor? If you do not have one, how can I serve you?

THINK WITH THE END RESULT IN MIND. THAT IS YOUR DESTINATION.

EMPOWERING BELIEF

CHAPTER NINE

REPETITION

Repetition, Repetition, Repetition is the mother of skill. It is essential to creating a vision that is so clear, so tangible that you can almost reach out and touch it. By now you understand the importance of having clearly defined goals written down on paper. I cannot emphasize enough the importance in doing this. Repetition is an integral part of the Success Formula.

The Success Formula is the progressive realization of a worthy idea. The bible says, "Delight thyself in the Lord: and he shall give you the desires of thine heart." Psalm 37:4 So, the key is desire. Desire + Skill x Faith = Success. Remove the t on heart and you get the word hear. I need to hear I am happy and grateful now that… minimally 10 times a day to develop desire in my heart. The goal is to inundate my mind with my desires. This turns your mind into a GPS to go where you have never been before. Why? Because you have made it important to your heart and mind. Eventually your mental GPS will bring you to the right people and the right opportunities to help you to achieve your goals. Write down your vision and make it plain. Your ability to act comes from what you see and hear every day. Print out 20 belief statements with images and strategically place them throughout your home with visuals. This is how you see it, hear it, touch it, and ultimately achieve it.

You need to look at it and read it every single day. You need to read your goals out loud every single day. You need to take that image from your future and make it into a reality every single day. If you do that once a day, you are in the top 3% of vision creators and goal writers in the world. The next step is execution, and it is truthfully such a simple step, yet it is often overlooked. In simplicity, repeatedly saying your burning desires or goals ten times a day is needed to properly execute this step. It is up to you. You could say it once a day or ten times a day impressing it upon yourself repeatedly. This is not new information. Spiritual teachers have shaped this concept for thousands of years. The rosary prayer bead necklace found in Catholic teachings have 59 beads in which prayers are recited repeatedly and counted on a knotted cord. Orthodox Christians count the number of times they have prayed using a prayer rope with thirty-three knots representing Christ's age at crucifixion. The Hindu's use 108 mala beads on a strand to recite mantras repetitively during meditation for the exact same

WE CAN BE ACTION TAKERS OR EXCUSE MAKERS, BUT NEVER BOTH.

reason. Repetition is the key to success. Remember the success formula; desire plus skills multiplied by faith equals success. Repetition of your desires is the first skill in this formula. "We can be action takers or excuse makers, but never both."- David Imonitie

REPETITION

EMPOWERING BELIEF

CHAPTER TEN

REDEMPTION STORY

As I study the bible, obviously there are many redemption sequences. That is ultimately what life is about. Living our lives to include moments of hardship or mistakes guided by the decision of making choices based on what is right or wrong. That experience is followed by deliverance from suffering. The lesson learned by experiencing hard times. These experiences shape everything about us, our personalities, our relationships, and our lives. The deliverance of your hard ship, how you came to know Jesus is your redemption story.

Being able to identify pivotal points of salvation in your life reinforces how much God loves us and wants a relationship with us. When God created the world, he saw everything he created and thought "It was very good". Genesis 1:31 This includes the creation of man. God wants to be the center of our lives and this is done through salvation. I am living proof of God's love and mercy.

One day, as I prepared to take my shower, I noticed a raised area approximately two inches located on the left side of my rib cage. I touched it, and it did not hurt. I sucked my stomach in, and it did not diminish. I felt nervous, not knowing what it was. I scheduled an appointment to see my primary care doctor and showed him. The doctor said, "Oh, that's nothing. It is called a lipoma, which means fatty tissue. No big deal." I said, "Are you sure?" The doctor said, "Well, the only way to be 100 percent sure would be to have it biopsied, but I see this all the time. Of which I usually can do the biopsy in the office. However, due to the size of your lump, I recommend outpatient surgery to have it biopsied." So that evening, I went home and contemplated whether I wanted to go through the outpatient surgery to have the lump biopsied. Something in my gut said, "Better safe than sorry." It was a quiet "What if?" voice. So, I decided, to relieve my mind of what it was or was not, I wanted to have the biopsy done.

The following week, I had the surgery and was released to go home afterward. While at home, I felt very weak and could not keep any food or fluids down. I vomited continuously. My mother told my husband she was concerned that I may become dehydrated and thought they should take me back to the hospital. When I arrived, the physician on duty asked me what

THE DELIVERANCE OF YOUR HARD SHIP, HOW YOU CAME TO KNOW JESUS IS YOUR REDEMPTION STORY.

caused me to become so sick. I responded that I had surgery earlier that day. The physician said, "What for?"

I was completely out of it and tried to tell him, "Lipoma." However, the physician must have misunderstood and heard "Lymphoma" because he ordered a bunch of x-rays and blood tests. They gave me IV fluids to make sure I was hydrated and released me to go back home.

A few days later, when I arrived at work, the message indicator on my desk phone was red, indicating I have messages to retrieve. The first message I listened to was from my primary care doctor, who asked me to call him as soon as I received the message. When I called the doctor back, he answered the phone and told me that I have cancer. He kept apologizing because he assured me that it was nothing; however, the x-rays showed different, and I needed to come back for further testing. I started crying hysterically. The people in the office who overheard my conversation gathered around me, asking if I was okay. I responded, "No, I'm not okay," and ran out of the office into the women's bathroom. When I got home, it was my husband who opened the door. The doctor had already broken the news to him. He was crying and said, "Debra, I'm so sorry. If I could take it from you, I would." That was one of the most beautiful and selfless things that someone could say. In 2000, I was diagnosed with cancer: lymphoma, which I had never heard of before. It felt like I was given a death sentence. When I was diagnosed, I was newly married about a year and a half and living in Orlando, Florida. The diagnosis was a complete shock because there was no history of cancer in my family. I underwent months of chemotherapy, followed by radiation therapy.

I lost a lot of weight and most of my hair, which I chose to just wear shaved low and naturally curly. Apart from that, the chemo made me extremely sick. To this day, I remember the smell of it. My mouth was sore. I did not have much of an appetite, and my body ached most of the time.

The hardest part for me was not losing my hair. It was the fear of dying. I remember my mother telling me to envision my body being healed. She said, "You have to see and know that God is healing you. While you receive your chemotherapy treatments, close your eyes, meditate, and visualize that a golden ray of sunlight is shining through your body layer by layer. Start with the crown of your head and see this healing light go all the way down to the soles of your feet. The light is warm, the light is powerful, and the light is healing and rebuilding your body from the inside out." I literally did this day after day while thanking God for the healing. I received God's healing. I expected God's healing. I prayed for the anointing over the doctors involved in my care. I prayed for the pharmacist who prepared the chemo. I prayed for the nurse who administered the radiation. I prayed for my strength to stay mentally and physically strong. I prayed for my husband's strength to stay by my side. I prayed for my parents' strength to handle seeing me go through this sickness. I prayed that one day I would be able to be a testimony of God's greatness and share my story with other people in hopes of helping someone else, and I have. Thank you, Father God!

My husband was incredibly supportive and took time off from work to attend all my chemotherapy treatments. Though it was difficult for my husband and parents to experience with me, they were by my side throughout it all. I thank God for the strength the Lord gave my family and me. I have been in remission for over fifteen years now. From this experience, I learned that no one is invincible. The last thing you think about in your twenties is the possibility of dying. I am proactive about my health and make sure that I follow up on all my doctor's appointments. I feel blessed to have a second chance at life. I forgot to mention, the raised area on my rib cage was lipoma or fatty tissue, just as the primary doctor said. The lymphoma was stage 3 and located inside my body. The external blemish was God's way of letting me know that something was wrong. The physician's mistake of hearing *lymphoma* when I tried to tell him *lipoma*—I have never heard of lymphoma before—was the Lord's divine way of letting the physician discover the sickness within. The Lord is utterly amazing and powerful in his way of showing us his grace. The cancer was not meant for my destruction but for my spiritual growth and testimony of the Lord's greatness.

In him we have redemption through his blood, the forgiveness of our sins, according to the riches of his grace which he lavished on us. Ephesians 1:7-8b

REDEMPTION STORY

EMPOWERING BELIEF

CHAPTER ELEVEN

THE WHEEL OF LIFE

They say, In life, you're either heading into a storm, going through a storm, or just coming out of a storm. Once my cancer battle was won, I decided I wanted to become a mother. We women have the gift of carrying and giving life through the miracle of childbirth. The only thing was I struggled with infertility issues. Apparently, the doctors explained that I may not be able to have children due to the cancer treatments, but at that time, I was only concerned with living. Nevertheless, I am one of those people that knew in my soul that I was destined to be a mother. It was extremely important to me and my husband, but more so to me. Not being able to become a mother would be like living an unfulfilled life.

EMPOWERING BELIEF

For years, my husband and I underwent almost every infertility test and treatment available, and then the doctors said, "At this point, the next option we need to consider is in vitro fertilization [IVF]." At that time, IVF costs about $20,000 for one cycle of treatment. Due to the cost and specialty nature, IVF was not considered a common treatment covered by medical insurance. We were living in Wisconsin due to my husband's executive career in the automotive industry, and I had a career in pharmaceutical sales. We had a six-figure household income, so if IVF was the next recommendation, there was no question on what we would have to do to become pregnant.

In 2007, we were blessed with the most precious little miracle, our daughter Alana. Having her is the most amazing gift of my life! My life is now complete. Our daughter is diagnosed with autism, ADHD and Down-syndrome. Many people are probably thinking, "Oh, man, their child is disabled." I want the world to know that I would not change a thing. My daughter is such a beautiful blessing. Alana was imperfectly and yet perfectly beautifully made just for us! She has given me so much happiness.

What I now understand is the wheel of life is always rotating through the different 8 areas of our lives. If desire is the reason why we do things, then our vision gives us the tangibility that shows us how to accomplish it. Therefore, it is imperative to hold a strong vision in every area of your life because each part influences the other. Picture your life as a wheelbarrow tire with 8 spokes. Each spoke represents an area of your life: health, finances, relationships etc. If one spoke breaks, it puts pressure on the other areas of our life. For example, I had difficulty conceiving a child which falls under the health category. To become pregnant, we had to rely on our finances to support our dream of becoming parents. Picturing our life as a wheel also helps us to have clarity, use objectivity while dealing with the pressures and stresses of life. The wheel on the barrel may look balanced but if you were to measure the stresses around the wheel than the part that is touching the ground is under significantly more pressure than the rest of the wheel. The pressure on this point is intense but it is also temporary. As life goes on, the wheel continues to turn, and the pressures shift. The pressures in our life work the same way. It is important to understand that everything is temporary." Whether good or bad, this too shall pass."- King Solomon. Health cycles goes through peaks and valleys. Financial pressures come and go. Relationship issues come and go. Every area of our life is constantly in motion. There is probably one area where you are feeling the pressure right now, just remember this too shall pass.

My mentor introduced me to the traffic light system which is an exercise used to track how your life is going. There are 8 elements that make up the wheel of life. These elements are split into two categories. The first category is the personal aspect to include health, personal growth, business or career and finances. So, for each of these aspects give them a rating from one to ten. 1-3 is a desperate situation, 4-7 is moderate and 8-10 means it is almost the best if not the best that it could be.

The second category is the external aspect which includes romantic relationship, whether you are with the love of your life or single right now. Other relationships to include family and friends. When rating this element take an average of family and friends together. The next element is fun and recreation. These are the outlets that bring you great joy that you get to experience on a regular basis. The last element is your physical environment. This one is extremely important. After rating each element that represents every area of your life, the next step is to know exactly where you need to focus. Using a red, orange, and green marker, highlight the elements so they really stand out.

"Success is doing ordinary things extraordinarily well." – David Imonitie

It is important to have an objective view of how all eight areas of your life are tracking in order to know exactly where you need to focus. For instance, highlight the areas where you are really lacking which are from 1-3 in red, highlight the elements in the middle orange and the areas where you are doing exceptionally well in green. Now you can see all areas in your life on one single sheet right in front of you. The last step is to find amazing balance.

Obviously, the red areas are where you need to put your focus. However, while focused on the read areas to try and increase your ratings it is equally important to also be aware of the orange areas, so they do not start to slip while majority of your focus is on the red area. Looking at your life right now, what are the red areas you need to be immediately focused on?

THIS TOO SHALL PASS. 2 CORINTHIANS 4: 17-18

This is a simple yet powerful activity that you can do every week, every month or at least 3-4 times a year that will give an accurate visual of where your life is right now and ensure that you are always on a path of growth. I personally conduct this evaluation monthly. Staying on the path to growth and on your way to success in the key to life!

THE WHEEL OF LIFE

EMPOWERING BELIEF

CHAPTER TWELVE

THE PEN IS MIGHTIER THAN THE SWORD

In today's age of technology, it is easy to use our laptop or hit record on some device to record our thoughts. However, I am an avid note taker and feel strongly that there is power in handwritten notes. The pen is mightier than the sword, it is also mightier than your keyboard. There is something fundamentally missing in the process of note taking that can only be achieved by putting a pen in your hand and making a physical connection to paper. I know this for fact because repetitive writing of notes is how I study and retained information throughout college. I still believe in handwriting notes today. Whether I am goal setting, journaling, or writing my daily gratitude when we put a pen in our hand and write on paper there is a psychological connection to the intention behind those words that we simply cannot get when our fingers are tapping random letters on a keyboard. Learning to write is often one of our first experiences in being praised for doing something considered a proper grown-up task.

When I became a mother, I had a life changing moment of clarity and love. I wanted to become the best mother for my daughter. As previously shared, my daughter was diagnosed with Autism (ASD), ADHD and Down syndrome. I completed a graduate program in Behavioral Intervention of Autism through UMASS Lowell. I committed to studying Behavioral Analysis because it is presently documented as the most effective approach to improving the lives of people diagnosed with autism and other related developmental disorders. This program was developed by UMASS Lowell's Psychology Department in collaboration with the Eunice Kennedy Shriver Center, which has been a pioneer in research, education, and service for people with developmental disabilities and their families.

It was so incredibly important to me that my daughter learned how to write that I became a handwriting advocate through the Handwriting without Tears program. Throughout our school aged years, it is a requirement to complete handwritten assignments. I noticed in elementary school, they just pass out papers and say, "copy this letter, write this sentence." There is no formal step-by-step instruction on how to properly formulate letters. A typical child will pick up a pencil and attempt it, whether the grip is proper or improper.

THE PEN IS MIGHTIER THAN THE SWORD

WRITE THE VISION AND MAKE IT PLAIN.
HABAKKUK 2:2

However, most children diagnosed with a neurological disability will not know where to start. I researched writing programs that teach letter formation with step-by-step instruction and have invested in the training to help my daughter comprehend how to properly formulate letters. My point is that comprehension of things is important, and we must seek help, get the knowledge necessary to overcome barriers and achieve success.

Psychologically it is a critical defining moment in our lives when we learn to write and that translates into an extremely powerful emotion and connection as we make our way from our adolescent to our adult years. In everything that you do from journaling to goal setting or taking notes on your daily success habits whenever it is physically possible to take a pen and hold it in your hand to write provides simple but clear insight that will have a profound impact in your outcomes. So, write it down, and make it plain!

THE PEN IS MIGHTIER THAN THE SWORD

EMPOWERING BELIEF

CHAPTER THIRTEEN

SURVIVE VS THRIVE

In February 2015, I lost my husband of seventeen years and the father of my daughter suddenly and unexpectedly due to health complications. He was only forty-four years old. Facing my husband's death was the hardest thing I ever had to go through. It left me shaken, miserable, afraid, alone, and confused. My biggest fear came into reality. All at once, I lost my life partner, the father of my child, the breadwinner of our family, and my confidant. So much of my life included this person and he was gone. Ever since that day my mind has operated in survival mode. I am now a widow, a single mother—solely responsible for rebuilding my daughter and my life. The fear of the unknown and all the responsibilities of life felt as if they were crippling me.

In 1943 Abraham Maslow first designed his hierarchy of needs which served as a visual representation of the stages all humans go through during their lifetime. What most people do not fully grasp is Maslow's hierarchy starts from basic survival needs and elevates to the ability to thrive. For people to evolve into a thrive experience we would have to change psychologically from a surviving mentality to a thriving mentality prior to experiencing a physical shift. Now if you think about, most successful entrepreneurs started from a place of pain, abject poverty, rejected at every turn, and fighting for survival so they would never have to experience that kind of pain again. You can take yourself from rags to riches based on your mind and what you believe. Oprah Winfrey is one of those people who sits at a table of self-made billionaires who share a similar story of being able to take their pain and turn it into a strength driven so deep by focusing all their energy to turn things around in all areas of their life. These people could also be referred to as pain avoiders. While my example referring to Oprah showed strength. Some people who are also considered paid avoiders handle it negatively by turning to alcohol and drugs to numb their painful experiences. In fact, over 80% of the population are driven by pain and therefor live in a state of survival mode. The reason this is significant, sometimes it is necessary to be in survival mode. But understand there is a limited amount of time that we can constantly operate on adrenaline before we break down either physically, mentally, or both. So, the key to success first and foremost is to decide when to psychologically shift from survive to thrive.

MASLOW'S HIERARCHY STARTS FROM BASIC SURVIVAL NEEDS AND ELEVATES TO THE ABILITY TO THRIVE.

Since my husband's death in 2015, I have mentally lived-in survival mode and just when I started to feel like I was making that mental shift out of it the COVID – 19 pandemic hit along with being diagnosed with cancer for the second time in my life which put me right back into survival mode again. I understand the entire world is experiencing unprecedented life changes and the unknown territory of dealing with the COVID-19 virus which is why now more than ever we must protect our energy. During these unprecedented times of crisis and chaos your mind and body cannot flourish in survival mode. Do not obsess in watching the news, media headlines and COVID updates. Instead commit to having faith over fear.

My mentor made a great point. He said, "If you have a roof over your head, food in your cupboards and a community that you belong to, then it is time for you to step out of survival mode and begin to thrive. We all have fears around the unknown, not being good enough, not belonging, and to some extent those fears never go away. For ninety-nine percent of the population who fear these things, it undermines every action that people take and they end up spending their whole lives in survival mode. Right now, is the time for you to switch from surviving to thriving". I have taken his advice and so should you. My experiences shared, tools and strategies in this book incorporated into your daily success habits can help you reshape your life forever. I am speaking from experience. Join me and make the conscious decision to make that shift from survival to thriving now, I know in my heart your life will never be the same.

SURVIVE VS THRIVE

EMPOWERING BELIEF

CHAPTER FOURTEEN

I FORGIVE MYSELF

The bible makes it clear that everybody needs forgiveness from God. It focuses on the preciousness of blood, the slaughter of sacrificial animals, the fire in the altar of burnt offering done before the Lord. The doctrine that humans were created in the image of God matters. Therefore, there are blessings of obedience and consequences for sins of disobedience.

As a widow, one of my greatest struggles is loneliness. The desire to have a companion. The desire to have support for my daughter and I outside of my parents. Being alone day after day causes depression, sadness, envy of others, and an occasional indiscretion outside of marriage which is a sin. At various points in my life loneliness has stolen my happiness. When I seriously think about it, I know God must think I am ungrateful because I am blessed beyond measure and yet I am complaining. I struggle with this and confessed to the Lord about it.

Father God, I humbly come to you and confess my sins of sadness, suffering in loneliness. I surrender this longing for love and companionship to you. Father I envy the lives of others on social media and often feel as if I am inadequate, not enough, I am fearful of the unknown of what my future holds resulting in constant anxiety and worry. Please forgive me. I surrender all my concerns to you; I trust you to care for me and my daughter in a perfectly loving way. Amen.

I started studying the bible to gain knowledge in what God wants to change in me. I realized the more I seek is actually God. Sanctification is accomplished when the word and the spirit work together. Although it is hard, part of taking care of my body and living Gods way includes committing to a sexually pure life. In my walk with Christ, I have listed seven strategies to living a sexually pure life.

Be careful of what I watch online and on television.

Find an accountability partner or mentor.

Walk away if they cannot respect my boundaries.

Journal about my experiences to see patterns and stay accountable.

Date men committed to avoiding sexual temptation.

Keep it casual, do not worry about how the relationship will manifest in the future.

INSTEAD OF FOCUSING ON PLEASING MAN, FOCUS ON PLEASING GOD.

Have a visual reminder or verbal saying if things start to heat up.

Now instead of focusing on pleasing man I am focused on pleasing God. God has a ministry for all of us to help others find Him. My transparency in this book is one way I can share my life experiences in hopes of helping someone else. We only have one earthly lifetime to try and reach as many people as possible with the gospel of our Lord and Savior Jesus Christ.

I FORGIVE MYSELF

EMPOWERING BELIEF

CHAPTER FIFTEEN

IMAGINATION

Society teaches every child that you must go to school, graduate from high school, and then go to college. After you graduate from college, you are to get a job working from 9:00 a.m. to 5:00 p.m. for a minimum of forty hours a week to pay your bills, save for retirement, and attempt to pay back thousands of dollars in outstanding student loan debt before you die. I was living the corporate-America way until…

In May of 2015, the HR Department of the company I worked for called me at home while I was out on family medical leave (FMLA) to notify me they were closing and that my medical benefits would end in one week. I thought, Oh my gosh! How much can I take? What's next?

After my husband's death, I still had my career for a couple of months, which is why I remained in South Florida. But now that my career ended, I had nothing keeping my daughter and me there. It was time to make another monumental decision. What do I do? Should I stay? Should I move? I made a drastic decision to move to another city closer to my parents. I discovered sometimes in life things happen because you are not living where God intended you to live. The minute you move into the new direction that God wants for your life; things fall into place. You start to feel better, you meet new people, opportunities start manifesting, life seems easier to navigate, you start to feel happier, you meet a different quality of people who are like-minded, and you learn to live a better quality of life. Yesterday is gone. We cannot get it back.

My career has always been in leadership, sales, and marketing. I have always been driven to exceed and committed to corporate America. Every corporation has a mission statement, business plan, and heavy sales goals to achieve as a company. I remember feeling incredibly stressed out with the goals associated with my careers. I trained, prepared, and was committed to achieving my individual as well as the overall company goals for years. It occurred to me that I do not want to follow society's rules regarding work anymore. Facing the death of my husband and trying to rebuild life for my daughter and me brought awareness of how fragile and precious time, health, and life itself really is. I want to spend my life making a difference in the lives of others, savor the essence of things, deeply love, increase my spirituality, connect to something much big-

IMAGINATION

ger and greater than myself, and live in the present moment of time and freedom.

Have you ever noticed that most cartoons and theme parks created for children involve using one's imagination? A visual action plan involves using your imagination and belief to create a greater version of your reality. People operating on a higher level are mentally unattached from reality. Think about inventors, those people who come up with inventions. They do not operate from a space of logic. What inventors have is the ability to conceptualize does not even exist yet. These people have the supernatural ability to tap into the unknown and bring it into reality. This is incredible! Are you wondering why some people can reach a higher level of consciousness more than others?

Imagination is the faculty or action of forming new ideas or images or concepts of external beliefs not present to the senses. Images refers to the life I truly desire, the fit body, optimal health, and finances. So, imagination is the ability of the mind to be creative or resourceful. I believe in revelation which means I have the ability to be creative. You were made in the image and likeness of God. God is the creator of the universe. For clarity, imagination is the faculty or action of forming new ideas which are words or images which are visuals or concepts which have emotional ties to the words and images in your mind. Either you believe the concept, or you do not believe it. External beliefs not present to the senses means you do not have to rely on your current situation, your current resources, your current bank account, or your current connections. Creation means bringing into existence not presently of the universe, especially when regarded as an act of God. Uni in universe means one and verse means words. In order for me to create this vision the words are critical. Therefore, expressing daily gratitude by saying "I am so happy and grateful now" brings God into existence. God is the word. "In the beginning was the Word, and the Word was with God, and the Word was God Himself. John 1:1

The bible also says, "God so loved the world, that he gave his only begotten Son," this means when you love you give. How do you give? Most people automatically think money but in addition to money there is time, resources, and wisdom. I desire to live a life of service glorifying God. I am so happy and grateful now that this book is helping to transform the lives of others through my experiences and wisdom shared. Ultimately, I know helping to transform the lives of others and creating a legacy for future generations to come is my divine purpose in life.

The question I asked myself is, "What do I want?" Many people have no idea what they want. They allow other people to dictate what they should aim for or do with their life based on what they are doing. Because what that person suggest has nothing to do with your true desires, you will feel unfulfilled. This question is not something that someone else can answer for you. You must answer this question for yourself and be specific. What do you want? Why do you want it? Look at your life and get real with yourself. For instance, someone might say, I want to be with someone who makes me happy. This statement fails the clear goal vision test of your future goals. The idea is to create a picture of your future goal so clear that

USE YOUR IMAGINATION AND BELIEF TO CREATE A GREATER VERSION OF YOUR REALITY.

it becomes tangible to you. Instead, your goal could be, I want to have a partner who is respectful, honest and lives with integrity, a partner who prides themselves in being physically fit, emotionally, and spiritually connected, a partner who is present and has their own unique goals and priorities. Now this is a highly specific picture of a real person and passes the clear goal vision test. A goal example might be, I want a lot of money. This goal fails the clear goal vision test because what does a lot of money mean? Instead say, I want ten thousand dollars in one-hundred-dollar bills which passes the test. It is detailed and specific enough that you could literally envision ten thousand dollars in stacks of one-hundred-dollar bills. The goal is to ignite every one of your goals into a burning desire which can only be done by knowing specifically what you want.

IMAGINATION

EMPOWERING BELIEF

CHAPTER SIXTEEN

THE LAW OF REPLACEMENT PRINCIPLE

Have you ever heard of the law of replacement principle? Everything in life has a place. When something is taken out of place, it must be replaced. Every tangible thing in life is replaceable. People are replaceable. Your home is replaceable. Your job is replaceable. Once you understand this concept, you can free yourself from material attachment. I believe in Christ. Christ makes up my belief system. What you believe in your heart, spirit, and mind is what will manifest in your life. As humans, we must constantly fuel our minds and belief system with empowering information.

If you are not plugged into something empowering that keeps your spirit consistently vibrating on a higher level, the universe will fill this void with something else that will break your spirit. I wish I made this up, but I did not, and if you think about it, it makes complete sense. This is the natural law of cause and effect. Keeping your emotions in check is critical. Whatever mind-set you create for yourself is what you will get. You must take responsibility for what you allow to impact your life. People often do not take responsibility for the chaotic situations that they create. I am still learning and practicing all of this. Have you ever mistreated or snapped at someone else because you were upset and acting emotional about another situation that had nothing to do with the person you just mistreated? I have been guilty of this many times. I take responsibility for acting out of emotion and allowing a situation to affect my mind-set and behavior. I had to break the cycle of flying off the handle when life throws an obstacle my way.

God is the only one in life that is perfect. If you want to access your God-given power, you must be fair, act impartial and unemotional to the things that happen in life. I am working hard to live my life on an accelerated level where I do not allow the actions of other people to hurt me or affect my mind-set or day in a negative way. I remember speaking to an acquaintance on the phone, and they asked how I was doing. I gave the "Hanging in there" response and returned the question. They responded, "My philosophy is 'I always have a good day no matter what.'"

I thought, Really, "no matter what"? Yeah, right. However, this response weighed heavily on my mind. It occurred to me that they were already taught to keep their emotions in check

TAKE RESPONSIBILITY FOR ACTING OUT OF EMOTION AND ALLOWING SITUATIONS TO AFFECT YOUR MIND-SET AND BEHAVIOR.

and focus on gratitude rather than a down-in-the-dumps attitude. Once I realized this, I was determined to adopt their philosophy too. It is natural to want to vent to other people about your problems and find the commonality that you are not alone in what you are going through.

However, choosing to repeat a negative situation repeatedly to other people only turns a molehill into a mountain. Then after you have gotten past the situation, people continually ask you about it. I now get that the tongue is powerful. The same way you repeated the negative situation you experienced, you could have spoken encouraging, positive solutions into the universe instead. In other words, ask yourself, "What can I do to make this situation better?"

We always have options in life. The goal here is to experience more of what you want in life. To accomplish this, you must speak it into existence. Too many people want to know the intimate details of what is going wrong in your life, and when you share, they have nothing worthwhile to say that comforts or even helps the situation. So why go there? The world is a negative place. The televisions are filled with daily news and reality shows that have a negative depiction of how life is lived. To get out of a negative mindset, I had to turn the television off and plug in to positive knowledge that feeds positive thoughts in my mind. I made the choice to change. My brain is moldable. I can reprogram my mind and shift my beliefs, habits, perceptions, thoughts, behaviors, and experiences from a negative place to a positive one. I choose to live life intentionally and at an accelerated level with the end goals of growth, love, real happiness, and contribution to the world in mind.

My parents repeatedly tell me to count my blessings and trust in the Lord. I waited patiently for the Lord to help me, and he turned to me and heard my cry. He lifted me out of the pit of despair, out of the mud and the mire. He set my feet on solid ground and steadied me as I walked along. He has given me a new song to sing, a hymn of praise to God. Many will see what he has done and be amazed. They will put their trust in the Lord. (Ps. 40:1–3, nlt)

EMPOWERING BELIEF

CHAPTER SEVENTEEN

POWERFUL LESSONS LEARNED

"As in the days of Sodom and Gomorrah" (Luke 17:28) is a verse my mother often remembers her father saying to her. The current state of the world runs parallel to biblical times filled with violence, pleasure-seeking, materialism, and rejection of Gods instructions. In other words, the wickedness of the world will continue to repeat itself until Christ returns.

The Israelites fear to enter the Promise Land led to a failure of trust in God. They complained the Amorites would destroy them as they were stronger, taller and their cities were larger with walls up to the sky. They did not trust God to fulfill his promises. Fear leads to disobedience which leads to sin and severe punishment. Because of this disobedience, the Israelites were barred from entering the Promise Land.

There are valuable lessons to learn from your experiences and the experiences of others. Isn't it interesting how frustrating situations continue to repeat themselves until we recognize our patterns of behavior that need to be changed or eliminated? Learning from past circumstances is what keeps you from repeating the same mistakes over and over again.

THERE ARE VALUABLE LESSONS TO LEARN FROM YOUR EXPERIENCES AND THE EXPERIENCES OF OTHERS.

EMPOWERING BELIEF

CHAPTER EIGHTEEN

BROKENNESS IS BEAUTIFUL IN GODS EYES

When God said in Proverbs 13:15, "The way of the transgressor is hard," no one was excluded from that principle – not even David, one of the greatest men to ever live; and in Psalm 51 we get a peek into that. We see a man truly broken by his transgression. God uses our desperation, heartbreak, grief, physical weakness, and spiritual brokenness to restore our heart, revive our body, renew our soul, and transform our lives to be led into fellowship with Him.

God wants sorrow that leads to reliance on Him and repentance from sin (2 Cor. 7:10). The reason brokenness is beautiful is because of how God can use it to transform us and glorify himself. Being broken is not lovely in and of itself, it is not the end of the journey, it is not a popular hashtag to put on a social media post. Brokenness alone, is messy, complicated, emotionally, and sometimes physically draining. The beauty of brokenness is found in your redemption story of grit, perseverance, healing, and triumph.

I learned that I am the solution to healing from my brokenness. As I have explored my daily success habits, I have been looking at the success formula and how to apply it to guide my journey. This life is not a rehearsal, it really is my journey. The problems that I face are mine, the wins are mine. The path that I walk of wins and losses belongs to me too which allows me to take 100 percent responsibility for my actions. Accountability for my outcomes is a very surreal realization that the path I have walked so far is a path of my own design. As a reminder the future path in front of me is my responsibility as well. The question is, am I going to walk the same path I have been where up to 80% of the actions and decisions have been unconscious or will I take charge, consciously create a better new path to take myself places I have never ventured to before. Right now, I have the tools inside of me to forge that new path, build my desire to a burning desire inside my heart. I can choose to increase the size of my dreams every day and chase them like I am living my last. I can make 1 percent, small incremental improvements that over the course of a lifetime compound into unbelievable heights, take action daily towards my dreams, create little wins every day. I can have faith through love and patience, enjoy the high, the wins while enduring the pains of the lows. Your faith

YOUR FAITH IN GOD AND ABILITY TO TAKE BOLD COURAGEOUS ACTION IS THE FINAL DETERMINING FACTOR IN YOUR JOURNEY TOWARDS SUCCESS.

in God and your ability to take bold courageous action is your final determining factor in your journey towards success. My purpose is to inspire and lift as I climb and teach others to succeed through my examples as a role model. It is such a blessing and privilege to share this amazing journey with you.

BROKENNESS IS BEAUTIFUL IN GODS EYES

www.ingramcontent.com/pod-product-compliance
Lightning Source LLC
Chambersburg PA
CBHW071730090426
42738CB00011B/2450